◆ Personal, Moral, So[cial]
and Cultural education

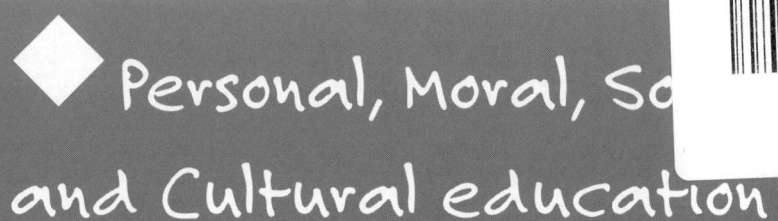

GROWING UP TODAY
People and communities

Key Stage 1/P1-3

Ros Bayley and Lynn Broadbent

HOPSCOTCH
EDUCATIONAL PUBLISHING

◆ Acknowledgements

Published by Hopscotch Educational Publishing Company Ltd, Althorpe House, Althorpe Street, Leamington Spa CV31 2AU.

© 1999 Hopscotch Educational Publishing

Written by Ros Bayley and Lynn Broadbent
Cover design by Kim Ashby
Page design by Steve Williams
Illustrated by Cathy Gilligan
Cover illustration by Cathy Gilligan
Printed by Clintplan, Southam

Ros Bayley and Lynn Broadbent hereby assert their moral right to be identified as the authors of this work in accordance with the Copyright, Designs and Patents Act, 1988.

ISBN 1-902239-18-0

All rights reserved. This book is sold subject to the condition that it shall not, by way of trade or otherwise, be lent, hired out or otherwise circulated without the publisher's prior consent in any form or binding or cover other than that in which it is published and without a similar condition, including this condition, being imposed upon the subsequent purchaser.

No part of this publication may be reproduced, stored in a retrieval system, or transmitted, in any form or by any means, electronic, mechanical photocopying, recording or otherwise, without the prior permission of the publisher, except where photocopying for educational purposes within the school or other educational establishment that has purchased this book is expressly permitted in the text.

Hopscotch ◆ People and communities KS1/P1–3

Contents

Introduction	4
What makes a community?	6
An urban community	11
An island community	16
An overseas community	21
An American community	26
Life on a canal	31
Living in two communities	36
At work and at home	41
Generic sheets	
If I could choose	46
What I would like	47
What a community needs	48

Introduction

As human beings we all have a fundamental need to belong to a community and to feel that we are able to make a strong personal contribution to that community. However, because most of us grow up as part of a community it is easy to take it for granted and fail to understand just how important being part of that community can be. For this reason, we felt that an exploration of communities should be an important part of the work of this series. Unlike the other titles in the series where the chapters can be used in almost any order, for the work on communities it is important to use Chapter 1 first, after which the chapters may be used in any order at the teacher's discretion. In Chapter 1 we have used a focus book with the specific intention of exploring the basic human need for a community, whilst the chapters that follow enable the children to consider what life might be like in a number of different communities. We have attempted to cover as diverse a range as possible. The key questions are aimed at encouraging the children to reflect upon a variety of issues relevant to an understanding of communities. For example:

◆ that there are certain prerequisites to the formation of a community

◆ that there are factors common to all communities

◆ that there are ways in which communities are different

◆ that there are different types of communities i.e. home, school, work

◆ that some people have more than one home/ community

◆ that the type of community in which we live has a considerable impact on our lives

◆ that most of us belong to a number of communities

◆ that a diverse range of communities exist

◆ that we all have responsibilities to the communities that we are part of

◆ that we have the capacity to both enhance or detract from those communities.

Communities are complex and the exploration of them is no easy matter, but if we can begin this process at an early age we can really help the children to begin to understand the vital role that communities play in their lives. When children comprehend this, they are far more likely to understand the ways in which they might contribute to the communities of which they are a part. Without this understanding we may be inhibited in our ability to contribute and if this happens we can never fully realise our human potential.

Through both belonging to and contributing to a community we gain security, fulfilment and happiness, so an exploration of communities and their functions should prove a very worthwhile experience.

BIBLIOGRAPHY OF TITLES REFERRED TO IN THIS BOOK

How Two-Feathers Was Saved From Loneliness by C J Taylor (Tundra Books)

Through My Window by Tony Bradman and Eileen Browne (Picture Mammoth)

Katie Morag Delivers The Mail by Mairi Hedderwick (Red Fox)

Hue Boy by Rita Phillips Mitchell/Caroline Binch (Gollancz Children's Paperbacks)

Jamaica Louise James by Amy West/Sheila White Samton (Walker Books)

Snowy by Berlie Doherty/Keith Bowen (Harper Collins)

Grace and Family by Mary Hoffman/Caroline Binch (Frances Lincoln)

Dear Daddy by Philippe Dupasquier (Picture Puffins)

What makes a community?

FOCUS BOOK

HOW TWO-FEATHERS WAS SAVED FROM LONELINESS
by C J Taylor
Tundra Books

INTENDED LEARNING

◆ To enhance the children's understanding of what a community is and why it is so important for us to be part of one.
◆ To enable them to see themselves as unique individuals.

Synopsis of the story

This story is a retelling of the legend 'The Origin Of Corn'. Two-Feathers has been wandering about by himself all winter and is feeling very lonely. In an attempt to forget his loneliness he lies down to sleep, to be woken by the voice of a beautiful woman calling his name. He tells her how lonely he is and says that if she will stay with him he will love her and look after her. She replies by saying that if he will trust her he will never be lonely again, so Two-Feathers follows her until they reach a meadow where she shows him how to make fire. She then tells him to pull her by the hair across the burned ground. Reluctantly he does this and when he has finished she has disappeared, leaving some green shoots behind. These grow into the first corn and it is not long before the people find it and a community is born.

Notes for teachers

This is an excellent book to use when undertaking an exploration of communities. It focuses sharply on what life feels like for someone who has no community and really helps children to understand why being part of a community is so important. We all need to belong to a group and feel that we can make a strong personal contribution to that group. At the beginning of the story Two-Feathers' sense of loneliness and isolation is very powerful and the evocative illustrations serve to heighten this feeling. Although it is a retelling of an ancient 'Abenaki' legend it is not difficult for even the youngest children to identify with Two-Feathers' need for human companionship. In using this book, it is important to clarify the children's understanding of a legend and talk about why, in the context of this legend, the world was a cold and lonely place.

Methodology

To help the children's understanding of this story it will be useful to have some corn on the cob that they can look at. It is even better if you can get it before it has been trimmed down and the silky threads are still round the corn. When you have first read the story with them ask the following questions.

Questions to ask

◆ What would it be like to spend all winter on your own? What would life be like and how would it be different to the way your life is now? What would you miss?
◆ Why was Two-Feathers so keen to follow the young woman?
◆ The young woman said that he must follow her. How do you think he felt when he was following her through forests and across streams?
◆ The young woman showed Two-Feathers how to make fire. Why was it important for him to be able to do this?
◆ She told him to pull her across the burned ground. How do you think he felt when he turned round and she was gone?
◆ Where Two-Feathers had pulled the young woman across the ground green shoots appeared and grew into the first corn ever grown. As the corn grew the people came to it. Ask the children why they think the people do this.
◆ The people built houses and a village in the place where the corn grew. Why did they do this?
◆ Do you think that Two-Feathers will be happy now? If so, why?

Encourage the children to identify the characteristics of a community. Show them the final illustration to help them to do this.

The photocopiable activity sheets

Belonging to a community The purpose of this activity sheet is to encourage the children to think about why a sense of belonging is so important to us. It is intended for children who cannot yet read independently and will need supporting through discussion and the shared reading of the 'feelings' words.

What we all need This activity sheet is intended to help the children to understand the most basic of needs of people within a community. The skilled use of open-ended questioning will help them to perceive the links between this concept and the pictures they draw.

Who lives in my community? This activity sheet is for children who can work independently. Before embarking on the drawing and writing activity they could work as a group to brainstorm the important people in their community.

Belonging to a community

◆ Think about how the child is feeling in the two pictures.

◆ Match these 'feelings' words to the pictures.

lonely

unhappy

happy

secure

afraid

loved

excited

sad

PHOTOCOPIABLE PAGE

Hopscotch ◆ People and communities KS1/P1–3

◆ What we all need ◆

◆ Draw pictures to show:

The way I keep warm.

The things I like to eat.

The friends I like to play with.

Hopscotch ◆ People and communities KS1/P1–3 PHOTOCOPIABLE PAGE

Who lives in my community?

◆ Draw some pictures of people who are important in your community. Write their names underneath the pictures. Write some sentences to say why these people are important.

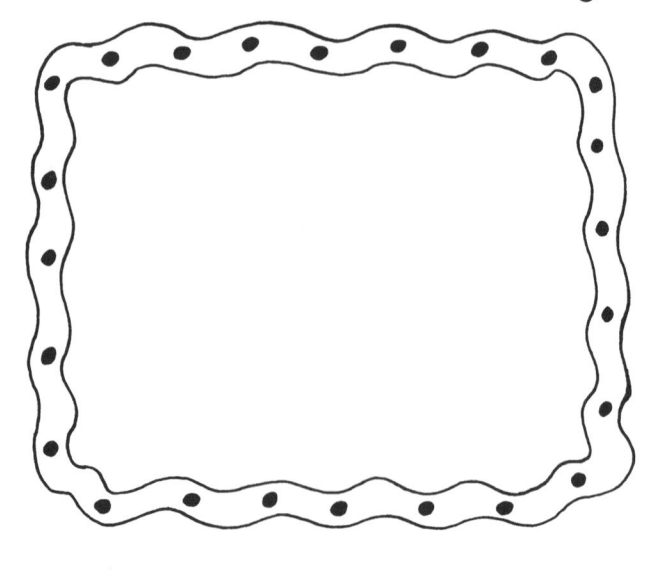

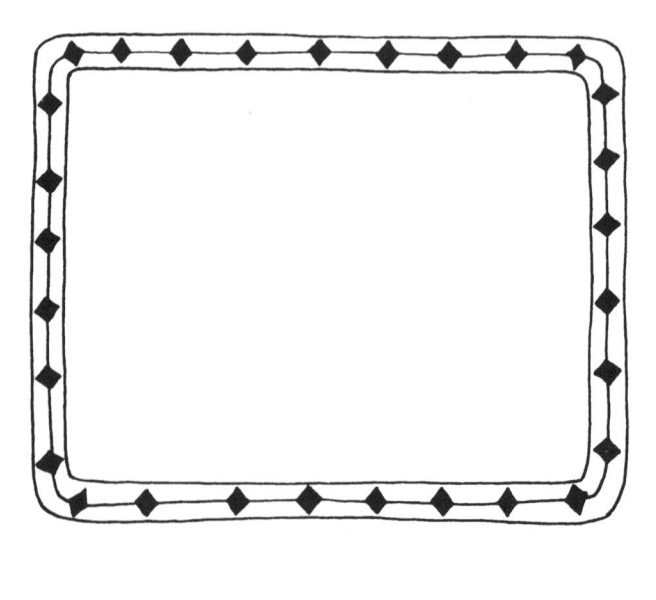

An urban community

FOCUS BOOK

THROUGH MY WINDOW
by Tony Bradman and
Eileen Browne
Picture Mammoth

INTENDED LEARNING

◆ For the children to explore what it may be like to live in a block of flats and notice similarities between the community presented in the book and their own.

◆ For the children to understand that living in a flat would be different from living in a house.

◆ To promote an understanding of the way in which there are certain people who are important to the life of a community.

Synopsis of the story

Jo has been ill in the night and wakes in the morning with a temperature. Her Dad tells her that she will have to stay indoors with him while her Mum goes to work. She wants her Mum to stay at home too but Mum says that she has to go to work. Mum leaves for work promising that when she comes home she will bring a surprise for Jo. All that day Jo waits impatiently for her Mum to return, jumping up to look through the window every time she hears a noise in the street. It is as she does this that we see the various activities that take place in her community. The story ends with Jo receiving the doctor's outfit she has always wanted.

Notes for teachers

Through My Window is set in a multi-ethnic urban community and provides the children with an opportunity to reflect upon the people that make up the community and are important to its existence. While some children will be able to identify with the setting it will be outside others' experience. The story provides a good context within which the children may consider how living in a flat may be different from living in a variety of other settings. An additional advantage of this book is the way in which it challenges certain stereotypes. For example, Mum goes out to work while Dad stays at home and the window cleaner is a woman. It is also one of the few books that unselfconsciously depicts a mixed race family.

Methodology

Having read the story to the class and examined the illustrations carefully, go on to ask a variety of questions and lead a class discussion on the following.

Questions to ask

- Can you think of a word to describe the type of house that Jo lives in? Which pictures tell you that Jo lives in a flat? Are all flats the same as the one Jo lives in? If you lived in a flat what would you like about it? What would you dislike?
- Jo doesn't want her Mum to go to work. Can the children think of some words to describe the way Jo is feeling? Why does she want her Mum to stay at home?
- Jo goes to sleep on the settee and wakes up when she hears footsteps coming up the street. Do you think that Jo has seen the postman before? What is it in the picture that tells you that they are friends? Do you ever talk to your postman or postlady?
- When the milkman arrives it is obvious that he knows Jo because he calls her by her name. Have the children got a milkman? Do they know who their milkman is? Have you ever spoken to him/her?
- After lunch, the next door neighbour brings some comics for Jo. Why do you think she has done this?
- Throughout the day Jo thinks about lots of things and meets lots of people but what does she think about most of all?
- Each time Jo looks out of the window she sees lots of different things. Can you name some of the things she sees?
- Just before the end of the story Jo is feeling really fed up. Why is she feeling this way? Think of some words to describe the way she feels about her present.
- Can you think of any reason why Jo has always wanted a doctor's outfit?
- How do you think Jo felt about the people she saw that day? Why are these people important and how might she have felt if she had not seen them?

The photocopiable activity sheets

Who are these people? This sheet is intended for children who are not yet reading independently. It is not simply a matching exercise and needs supporting with discussion. Its purpose is to help the children think about the wide range of people to be found in a community.

Who do you see? This activity is a little more demanding and requires the children to write some words on their own. It is intended to stimulate their thinking about people in the community.

Living in a flat This sheet is intended for children at a more advanced stage of development. It requires reflective thinking and the ability to write independently.

Who are these people?

◆ Match the pictures to the words.

postlady

window cleaner

rubbish collector

nurse

lollipop lady

doctor

Hopscotch ◆ People and communities KS1/P1–3 PHOTOCOPIABLE PAGE

◆ Who do you see? ◆

◆ The postman or postlady visits everyone's house.

◆ Draw pictures of other people you see in your community. Write their names under the pictures.

◆ Living in a flat ◆

◆ Do you live in a flat? If you don't, can you imagine what it would be like to live in one? What would be good and what would not be so good? Write your ideas in the boxes below. Two have been done for you.

Good things	Not so good things
◆ A super view	◆ No garden
◆	◆
◆	◆
◆	◆
◆	◆

◆ Now write a list of the people you see from your window.

◆ An island community

FOCUS BOOK

KATIE MORAG DELIVERS
THE MAIL
by Mairi Hedderwick
Red Fox

INTENDED LEARNING

◆ For the children to explore the implications of a small island community and consider how Katie Morag's life may be different from their own.

◆ To enhance the children's understanding of the ways in which different things are important to different communities.

Synopsis of the story

Katie Morag lives on a small island where her family own the shop and post office. On the day of the story everything is in chaos and to make matters worse the boat has just brought mail and provisions from the mainland. Katie Morag is given the job of delivering the parcels to each of the five houses on the island. Unfortunately, as she stops to paddle in a pool, the mail bag falls into the water and by the time she retrieves it the labels on the soggy parcels are unreadable. As a result of this unfortunate accident all the parcels are delivered to the wrong houses, but with her Grannie's support, Katie Morag sorts the problem out and her family never know a thing about it!

Notes for teachers

The small community featured in this book is one with which very few children will be able to identify. The purpose of using this book is to provide them with an opportunity for reflecting on what life might be like in a community that is completely different from their own. Katie Morag Delivers The Mail provides an excellent context for considering what life may be like in a very small, remote community. An additional bonus is in the portrayal of Katie Morag's Grannie, who is a capable lady who lives alone and drives a tractor.

Methodology

Before discussing the story with the children it is important to clarify their understanding of what an island is. It may be helpful to look at the map on the first page and check out that they understand terms such as 'mainland' and 'jetty'. Allow the children to have another look at the illustrations and ask them.

Questions to ask

- How is this place different from the place where you live?
- How do you think Katie Morag's life would be different from yours?
- Why was Wednesday a special day?
- What would have happened if the boat hadn't come?
- Katie Morag is allowed to go out all on her own. Why do you think that it is all right for her to do this?
- Katie Morag spends a lot of time on her own. Why do you think this is?
- Katie Morag was asked to deliver the mail. Would you ever be asked to do anything like this?
- How do you think Katie Morag felt when all the mail fell into the pool?
- Katie Morag threw any old parcel at the houses. Why do you think she did this?
- When she told Grannie all about what had happened, Grannie expected her to sort it out for herself. Do you think this was fair?
- Show the children the picture of the 'holiday people' and ask them how this family is different from the other people that live on the island.
- Katie Morag's Grannie drives a tractor. Why do you think she needs a tractor? Do many people have Grannies who drive tractors?
- Why you think that Katie wanted Grannie to go back with her for tea?
- What do you think Katie expected to find when she arrived home?
- What do you think about Katie Morag's life? Would you like to live on a small island as she does?

The photocopiable activity sheets

Make an island This sheet is intended to help children think about things that would be seen on a small island and things that would not. It should support their thinking about why communities are different.

Island people This activity is for children who are not yet recording in words. Its purpose is to help them to think about the differences between a small island community and other sorts of communities.

Living on an island To complete this activity the children need to be able to write independently. It is intended to help them think about the ways in which the activities we engage in are often governed by the type of community in which we live.

Make an island

◆ Draw and label the things you would see on an island.

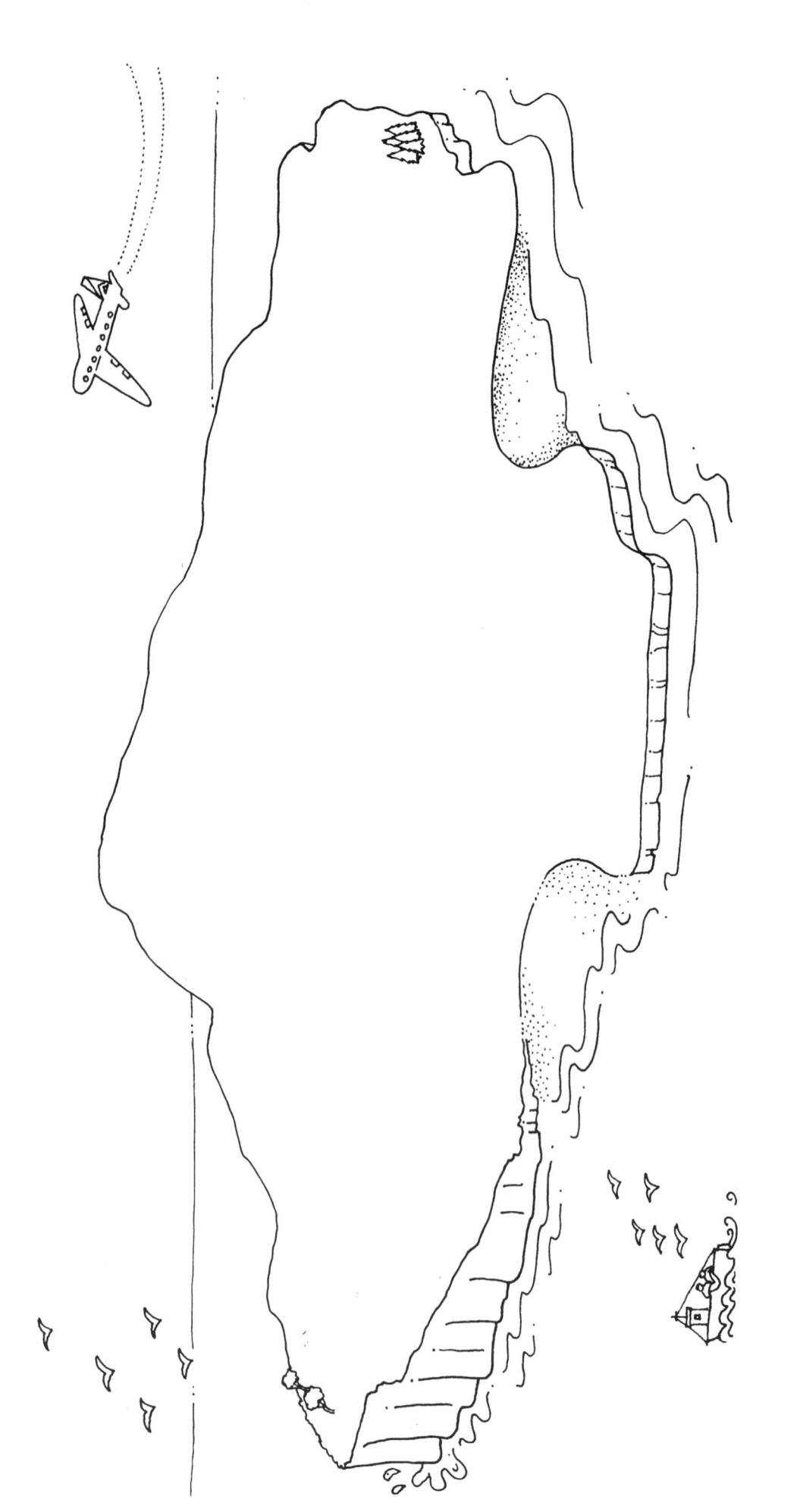

◆ Island people ◆

- Cut out these pictures and put them into two groups:
  Group 1 – People you would see on a small island.
  Group 2 – People you would not see on a small island.

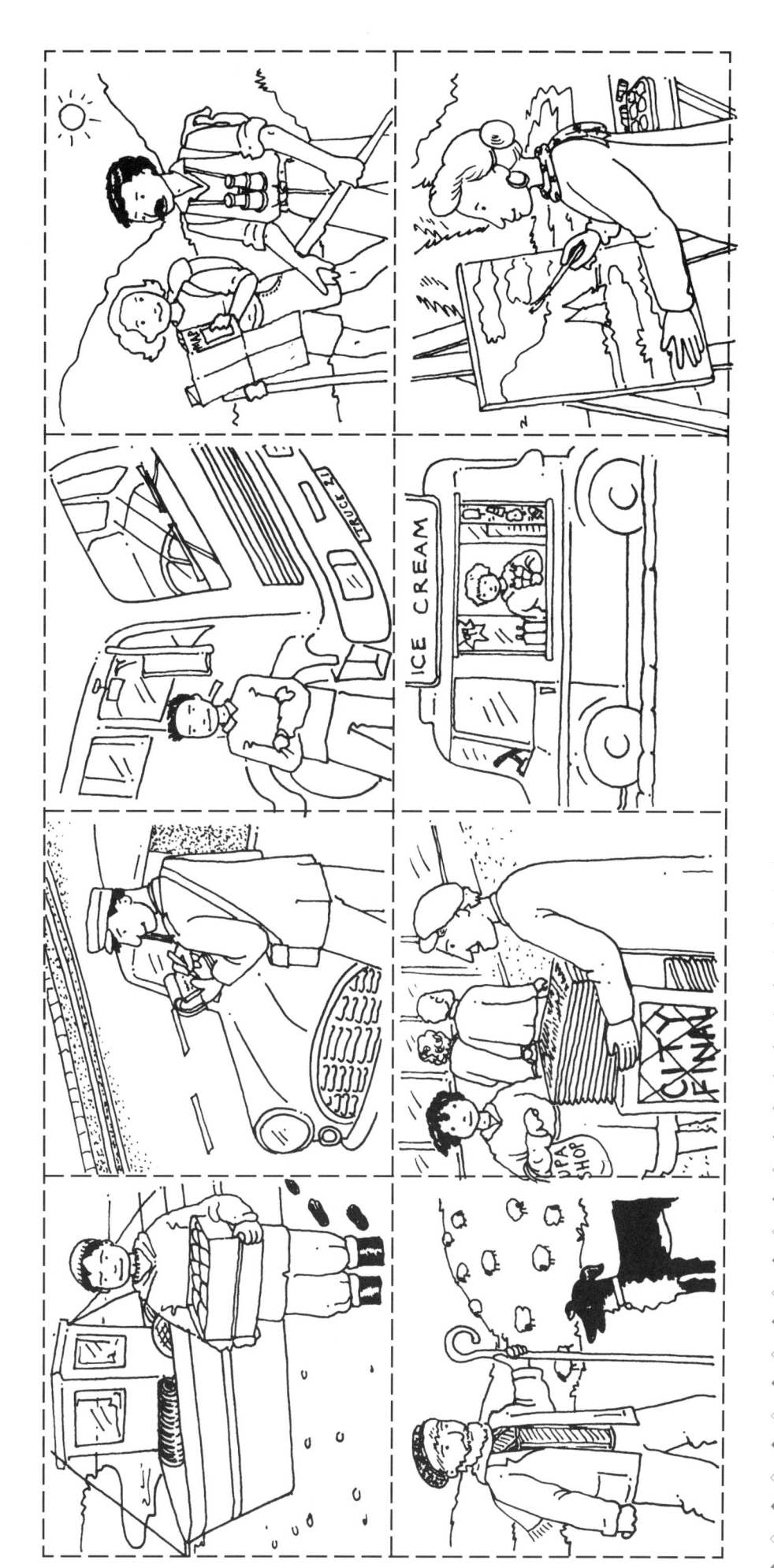

Hopscotch ◆ People and communities KS1/P1–3   PHOTOCOPIABLE PAGE   19

◆ Living on an island ◆

◆ Draw two things you could do if you lived on a small island.

◆ Draw two things you could not do if you lived on a small island.

◆ Write some sentences to describe how you would feel if you lived on a small island.

_____

_____

_____

_____

An overseas community

FOCUS BOOK

HUE BOY
by Rita Phillips Mitchell and
Caroline Birch
Gollancz Children's
Paperbacks

INTENDED LEARNING

◆ For the children to explore what life may be like in a Caribbean village and consider ways in which it may be different from life in their community.
◆ To consider ways in which the type of community, including the people, in which we live can impact on our lives.

Synopsis of the story

Hue Boy is an engaging and beautifully illustrated story set in a Caribbean village. Hue Boy's big problem is that he is so small that all his friends and classmates tower over him. His mother is very concerned about him. She measures him every morning before he goes to school and feeds him pumpkin soup in the hope that it will make him grow. When this fails she seeks the help and advice of a neighbour, the local wise man, the doctor and the healer, but it is not until his father returns home from working on a big ship that Hue Boy finally starts to grow.

Notes for teachers

This story provides the children with the opportunity of exploring a community that will be very different from their own. In the small Caribbean village where Hue Boy lives, the buildings, the lifestyle, the roads and the natural environment will be in sharp contrast to the experience of most British children. However, there will be some children who have relatives who either still live in such a community or can remember a time when they did. Through working with this story the children will be able to consider ways in which people's diet and lifestyle can be dictated by the type of community in which they live and where it is situated. They will also enhance their understanding of the way in which different people are important to different communities. Hue Boy also enables us to explore how it may feel to be different and the effect that this may have on the people that love us.

Methodology

Before discussing this story with the children it will be beneficial to carry out a certain amount of preparatory work. Show them where the Caribbean is on a globe or map and talk about the way the weather, the food and so on may be different to our own. It may be helpful to take some items such as mangoes and guavas into school and ask the children if they would like to eat the same kind of food as Hue Boy. Do they think Hue Boy will have a chip shop and McDonald's where he lives? Let them look at the illustrations again and ask the following questions.

Questions to ask

- What looks different about Hue Boy's house, his garden, his clothes?
- How do you think that he feels about being much smaller than all his friends?
- How does his Mum feel about him being so small? What does Mum think he needs to make him grow?
- How do you think Hue Boy feels about his Dad working on a big ship far away from home?
- How does 'Granma' try to help?
- What does the neighbour think will help Hue Boy to grow taller?
- Mum says that they should look for help in the village. Who does she go to first?
- Have you got a wise man in your community?
- Who were the other people in the community that tried to help Hue Boy?
- For one whole month Hue Boy tries out everybody's suggestions, but still he grows no taller. How do you think he feels about this?
- Did Hue Boy recognise his Dad when he first saw him at the end of the story? How did he feel about his Dad being back?
- Show the children the illustration of the people in the community. Why do the children think they are all looking happy?
- Do you think Hue Boy knows all the people that live in his community?
- Do you know all the people in your community?

The photocopiable activity sheets

Who would help you? This sheet requires no written recording. It is intended to help the children think about who is available to help them in their community and to consider ways in which Hue Boy's community is different from their own.

Which goes where? This activity will help the children to explore the differences between a Caribbean village and an urban community. It requires no written recording.

A Caribbean village This activity is intended for children who can work independently. Its purpose is to help them to explore what it might be like to live in a Caribbean village.

◆ Who would help you? ◆

◆ In the story Hue Boy was helped by the neighbour, the local wise man, the doctor and the healer. Who would help you in your community? Draw two of those people here.

◆ Look at this picture of a Caribbean community. Talk with a friend about how your community is different from Hue Boy's.

◆ Which goes where? ◆

◆ Cut out these pictures and sort them into two groups:
Group 1 – Things you would find in a Caribbean village.
Group 2 – Things you would not find in a Caribbean village.

24   PHOTOCOPIABLE PAGE   Hopscotch ◆ People and communities KS1/P1–3

◆ A Caribbean village ◆

◆ Look carefully at this picture.

◆ Now write some sentences to say what you think would be good about living in a Caribbean village.

_____
_____
_____
_____
_____
_____
_____

An American community

FOCUS BOOK
JAMAICA LOUISE JAMES
by Amy West and Sheila White Samton
Walker Books

INTENDED LEARNING

◆ For the children to explore what it may be like to live in a very large city and understand that for people to feel a sense of community, communication needs to take place.

◆ To enhance the children's understanding of the way in which one individual can have an impact on a community and be a catalyst for change.

Synopsis of the story

Jamaica Louise James lives in New York with her Mama and 'Grammy'. She loves to spend her time drawing, painting and telling stories about all the things she sees around her. Grammy works in a subway, where everyone scurries about frantically and nobody really communicates. When Jamaica has a new set of paints for her birthday she has a big idea for cheering Grammy up. Over a period of time she paints pictures of all the people Grammy describes from the subway. On the morning of Grammy's birthday, she and Mama take the paintings and put them up all over the walls of the subway station. Grammy is delighted and before long, the pictures have got everybody talking and smiling.

Notes for teachers

This book provides an excellent opportunity for exploring what life might be like in one of the biggest cities in the world, but it is important for the children to understand that not all American communities are like New York. Jamaica Louise James is probably best used with children aged around six or seven, but it is possible to use it with younger children if you tell the story and explore the illustrations. The book provides a context within which children can consider what it may be like to see the same people every day, but never really get to know them. Within this community, people are acquainted with each other on a very different basis. Jamaica Louise's Grammy knows people as 'Lady with green hat' or 'Gentleman with blue bow tie'. This is a story that tells of how a small child can have a genuine impact on a large anonymous community.

Methodology

Discussion of this story is almost sure to require some preliminary scene-setting. Show them the illustration of the skyline and check that they know what a subway is and why subways are to be found in big cities. The language in this book is quite idiomatic and may need some explanation.

Questions to ask

- Explore the character of Jamaica. Ask the children what Jamaica had for her birthday and why it was so important to her.
- What sort of things does she like drawing and when does she do it?
- Clarify the children's understanding of what Grammy does for a living. Ask them where Grammy works and what she does. Why does she leave for work while it is still dark? What does she do when she comes home?
- Why doesn't Jamaica like the subway stations?
- Why do you think the people look cross?
- What do Jamaica and Mum do on the morning of Grammy's birthday?
- Why do you think Jamaica wanted to do this?
- What sort of pictures has Jamaica painted?
- What gave her the ideas for the pictures?
- What does Grammy think about the pictures?
- What happens when all the people see the pictures?
- Look at the pictures of the subway before and after Jamaica has put up her pictures. Which do you like best?
- Would you like to live in New York? How might it be different from where you live?

The photocopiable activity sheets

An American subway This activity sheet is for children who are not yet recording in writing. Encourage them to discuss the picture and perhaps compare it with their own experiences.

Describe the subway In this activity the children have to make the subway appear a more cheerful place in which to be and then to choose some words to describe the subway and its community.

What do they think? This sheet is intended for children who can imagine what other people might be feeling about their community or environment and then to write some speech about how they and the different people feel.

◆ An American subway ◆

◆ Look at this picture of an American subway station. Talk to your friend about the picture. Draw yourself and your friend in the picture.

◆ Describe the subway ◆

◆ Look at this picture of an American subway. Draw yourself in the picture. Draw some pictures on the walls to make it look cheerful.

◆ Write some words in the boxes to describe the picture.

Hopscotch ◆ People and communities KS1/P1–3   PHOTOCOPIABLE PAGE   29

◆ What do they think? ◆

◆ Look at this picture of an American subway station. Write inside the speech bubbles what you think the people are saying about the subway.

◆ Draw yourself in the picture with a speech bubble. Write inside the speech bubble what you think of the subway.

◆ On the back of this sheet draw a picture of a subway that is much more cheerful.

Life on a canal

FOCUS BOOK

SNOWY
by Berlie Doherty and
Keith Bowen
Harper Collins

INTENDED LEARNING

◆ To enhance the children's awareness of the way in which children who belong to the same school community may have diverse home communities.

◆ To promote an understanding of what it might be like to live in a community that is very different from that of their peers.

Synopsis of the story

Rachel lives in a narrow boat and when her class have a 'pet's day' she is desperate to take Snowy, the boat horse, to school. Her mother has other ideas and says that she cannot do this because a boat horse has to work for a living and is not a pet. Rachel is bitterly disappointed and ends up in tears. What she doesn't realise is that Miss Smith, her teacher, has been to her parents and secretly arranged for her class to visit the canal and meet Snowy. The next day, instead of having a story at the end of the day, Rachel's class go on a walk, which culminates not just in meeting a boat horse but gives them the added bonus of a trip on the narrow boat.

Notes for teachers

Snowy offers us the opportunity of exploring both a home and a school community. The children are able to consider what life may be like for someone living in an unusual community. Although Rachel lives on a narrow boat that can move from place to place, she is still very much part of a community and as the story proceeds we get glimpses into the lives of people who live and work on the canal. The story also enables the children to explore the feelings of someone who finds themselves in a community that is very different from that of their peers. When this happens to children they can feel very isolated. Fortunately for Rachel, the little girl in this story, her teacher sensitively intervenes and arranges a meeting of the two communities. Consequently, Rachel feels included and her peers are able to gain insight into the community in which she lives.

Methodology

This story is full of descriptive language and presents children with a lot of information to assimilate. For this reason, having once read the story it may be necessary to flip backwards and forwards so that they may clarify and consolidate their ideas.

Questions to ask

- How do you think Rachel's life will be different from yours?
- How do Rachel's Mum and Dad earn a living?
- Why wouldn't Rachel's Mum let her take Snowy to school?
- Why did Rachel find this so upsetting?
- When Rachel described her pet to the other children, did they understand what she was talking about? (It may be necessary to re-read Rachel's description of Snowy.)
- Why do you think Miss Smith visited the canal to talk to Rachel's Mum and Dad?
- When the people that live on the narrow boats have finished working how do they spend their time?
- What happens in your community on a summer evening?
- How did Rachel feel when the other children went to see her home?
- What did her friends think about Snowy?
- Why was it so important to Rachel that her friends saw Snowy?
- Encourage the children to look carefully at the illustrations of the canal and think about what it might be like to be part of this community.
- Get the children to reflect upon how Rachel might be feeling at the end of the story. Ask them:
    - How does Rachel feel about her classmates visiting the canal? Has this been important to her?
    - Can you think of anyone else who lives in an unusual community?

The photocopiable activity sheets

The right community This sheet requires the children to recognise different communities and the people who might be found there. This is suitable for children who are not yet recording in writing.

Your school community This activity requires the children to think about the friends that are important to them within their school community.

A community for you This sheet is intended for children who can write independently. Again, the emphasis is on the differences between communities and their relative advantages and disadvantages.

◆ The right community ◆

◆ Draw lines to match these people with their communities.

Hopscotch ◆ People and communities KS1/P1–3   PHOTOCOPIABLE PAGE

◆ Your school community ◆

◆ Draw pictures of some of the children in your school community. Write their names underneath.

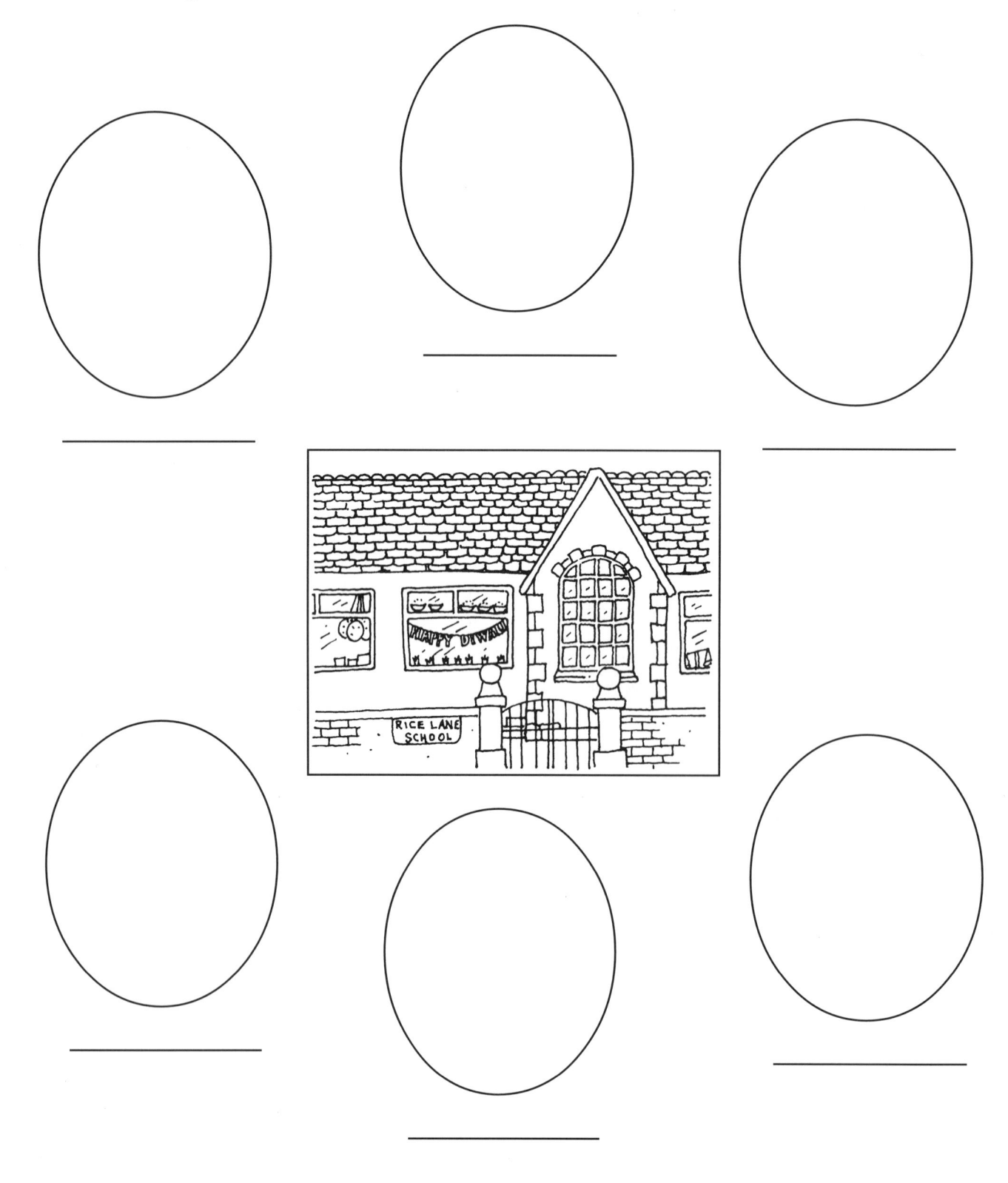

34   PHOTOCOPIABLE PAGE   Hopscotch ◆ People and communities KS1/P1–3

◆ A community for you ◆

◆ Look at these pictures of two different communities. Choose one of them and write some sentences to say what you would like about it if you lived there.

_____
_____
_____
_____
_____
_____
_____
_____
_____
_____

◆ Now choose a different community that you would like to be part of. Draw a picture and write about it here.

_____
_____
_____
_____
_____

Hopscotch ◆ People and communities KS1/P1–3   PHOTOCOPIABLE PAGE   35

Living in two communities

FOCUS BOOK

GRACE AND FAMILY
by Mary Hoffman and
Caroline Binch
Frances Lincoln

INTENDED LEARNING

◆ To increase the children's awareness of the way in which people can belong to one community and have roots in another, sometimes very different community.

◆ To help the children to understand that belonging to more than one community is not always easy.

Synopsis of the story

This is the sequel to Amazing Grace. Grace lives with her Ma, her Nana and a cat called Paw-Paw. She loves stories and is especially fond of those with fathers in, as her own father went back to Africa when she was born. Then one day when Grace comes home from school she finds that her father has sent the money for two tickets to visit him in the Gambia and that Nana has offered to go with her. When they arrive at the airport Grace is not even sure that she will recognise her Papa. The rest of the story revolves around Grace discovering her 'other' family and a new community and culture. This presents her with a variety of conflicts but by the time she returns home she has finally accepted that families don't necessarily have to be like the ones in her story books.

Notes for teachers

This is a story about a young girl discovering her roots. It explores the feelings of a child who has experienced the separation of her parents in a dramatic way. The community to which her father has returned is very different to the one in which she lives and discovering this new community involves Grace in managing a range of difficult feelings. Her concept of a family is the stereotypical one of a mother, a father, two children, a cat and a dog. So in addition to acting as a vehicle for the exploration of what it might be like to belong to two communities, this story provides an opportunity for looking at the structure of families and their diversity. For many children, having to adjust to belonging to two different communities can be a difficult and confusing experience. Grace and Family deals with these difficulties with frankness and sensitivity and promotes a real understanding of the complexities of such a situation.

Methodology

To make the fullest possible use of this book it needs to be used in conjunction with 'Amazing Grace'. When the two books are used side by side, the children are able to make comparisons between Grace's own community and the one she discovers when she visits her father in the Gambia. The beginning of the book looks at Grace's ideas about families in general and fathers in particular and it is important to clarify the children's understanding in this respect.

Questions to ask

- Why did Grace feel that her family was not 'right'?
- How do you think Grace felt when her Papa sent her the money to visit him in Africa?
- When Grace first arrived in the Gambia how were things different? (Encourage the children to look closely at the illustrations to help them to answer this question.)
- When Grace and Nana arrive at her Papa's house how are the clothes different from the clothes of her 'other' family?
- When Grace is staying with her other family will she eat the same food as when she is at home?
- Grace goes shopping with her father. How might this be different to shopping in Great Britain?
- Grace chooses material for her first African dress. How do you think she feels about this?
- As Grace gets to know her 'other' family how does she feel about having two families?
- On her last morning in Africa, Papa takes Grace to see some crocodiles and she makes a wish. What do you think she wishes for?
- When it is time to go home how does Grace feel about leaving her family in Africa?
- What do you think Grace has learned from her visit to the Gambia?

The photocopiable activity sheets

Things I do in my community This sheet will need supporting with much discussion but requires no written recording.

Two communities The purpose of this sheet is to encourage the children to think about what it may be like to spend time in two diverse communities and what they may like or dislike about this. They may need to be supported in reading the statements.

Two different lives This sheet is intended for children at a more advanced level who are able to imagine different situations and make informed decisions.

Things I do in my community

◆ Can you do these things in **your** community?

◆ Draw pictures to show some of the things you can do in your community. What would it feel like to have to go somewhere where you could not do these things?

◆ Two communities ◆

◆ Look at these two pictures of different places.

◆ Imagine that you live half the year in one of these places and the other half of the year in the other. Put a ✔ by those things that you would like. Put a ✘ by those things that would not be so good.

You live with different people. ☐

You can stay in two places. ☐

You travel between two homes. ☐

You have lots of friends. ☐

You eat different food. ☐

You meet lots of different people. ☐

You play different games. ☐

You have to leave your 'other' family behind when you go. ☐

You wear different clothes for each place. ☐

◆ Two different lives ◆

◆ Look at these two pictures of different places.

◆ Imagine that you live half the year in one of these places and the other half of the year in the other. Write some sentences to describe what you would like and what you would not like about having two different lives. Use the sentences in the box to help you.

_____

_____

_____

_____

_____

_____

_____

| ◆ You live with different people. |
| ◆ You can stay in two places. |
| ◆ You travel between two homes. |
| ◆ You have lots of friends. |
| ◆ You eat different food. |
| ◆ You meet lots of different people. |
| ◆ You play different games. |
| ◆ You have to leave your 'other' family behind when you go. |
| ◆ You wear different clothes for each place. |

At work and at home

FOCUS BOOK

DEAR DADDY
by Philippe Dupasquier
Picture Puffins

INTENDED LEARNING

◆ For the children to understand there are home communities and work communities and that for some people, the work they do involves them in being away from their home community for long periods of time.

◆ For the children to understand the impact that such circumstances have on individuals and families.

Synopsis of the story

Sophie's father works far away at sea on a freighter and as the title suggests Dear Daddy takes the form of a letter Sophie writes to her father to tell him about the interesting things that are happening at home. The story spans all four seasons of the year and the illustrations contrast Sophie's life at home with the very different life of her father's working environment. This is a story of everyday life in two contrasting communities, which ends happily when Sophie's father finally returns home.

Notes for teachers

For most adults, their working life takes up an average of eight hours a day but for Sophie's father, he is in his working environment for twenty four hours a day for a whole year. Through exploring Dear Daddy it is possible for the children to build up an idea of what life may be like for someone working a long way from home. They will be able to think about all the things that someone in this position might miss and examine the differences between a home community and a work community. With help, they should be able to appreciate the emotional impact that such a situation will have on a family and understand the importance of communication between the communities.

Methodology

In discussing this book it is important to clarify the children's understanding of its format. Discuss why the book is called Dear Daddy. Explain the terms 'air mail', 'able seaman', 'eternity' and 'c/o'. They may also need help in understanding the way in which the book deals with two parallel storylines.

Questions to ask

- What does Sophie's Dad do?
- How does Sophie feel about her Dad working away from home?
- How does she keep in touch with him?
- Talk to the children about the people in Sophie's community. Ask them:
    - Who are the people that come to Sophie's house?
- Who are the people in Dad's community?
- What are the differences between the two communities?
- How do you think Dad gets Sophie's letters?
- Would there be a doctor or a dustbin man on Dad's ship?
- What would be difficult about spending all that time away from home on a big ship?
- How do you think Dad feels about being away from home for such a long time?
- What do you think are the things that he would miss most of all?
- How do you think Sophie's Mum might feel about Dad being away from home for so long? How would this affect her life?
- Will it mean that she has more jobs to do in the home?
- What do you think Dad will like best about coming home?
- Encourage the children to think about how they would feel if they had to be away from home for a long time. Some children may have experienced this and may be willing to share their experiences.

The photocopiable activity sheets

Different communities This activity requires no written recording and is intended to help children begin to understand the ways in which we can belong to several different communities.

Work communities This sheet is intended to get the children thinking about the implications of working a long way away from home. They will only need to write the words 'near' or 'far away'.

My school community This sheet is intended to help the children consider the importance of their school community. It requires them to write independently.

◆ Different communities ◆

◆ Cut out the pictures and put them into three groups:
Group 1 – Things you would see in a home community.
Group 2 – Things you would see in a school community.
Group 3 – Things you would see in a work community.

Hopscotch ◆ People and communities KS1/P1–3   PHOTOCOPIABLE PAGE   43

◆ Work communities ◆

◆ Look carefully at each picture and decide whether the person works near to home or far away from home. Write your answers under each picture.

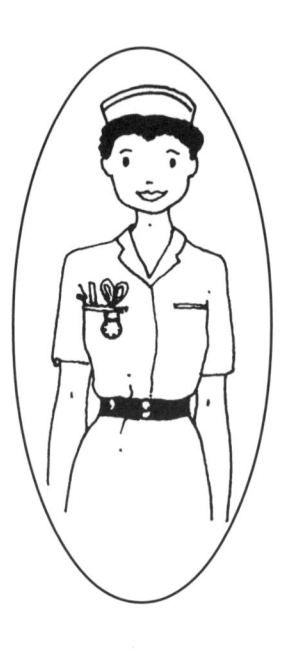

PHOTOCOPIABLE PAGE

◆ My school community ◆

◆ Imagine you are away from school for a long time.

◆ Write some sentences to describe:
  – the people you would miss
  – the things you would miss most

_____
_____
_____
_____
_____
_____
_____
_____

If I could choose

◆ In which community would you most like to live? Cut out the pictures and put them in order. Start with the community you would <u>most</u> like to live in.

◆ Talk to a partner about your choice of communities.

46 PHOTOCOPIABLE PAGE Hopscotch ◆ People and communities KS1/P1–3

What I would like

◆ Draw pictures of things you would like to have in a community. Think carefully about all the things you and your family would need.

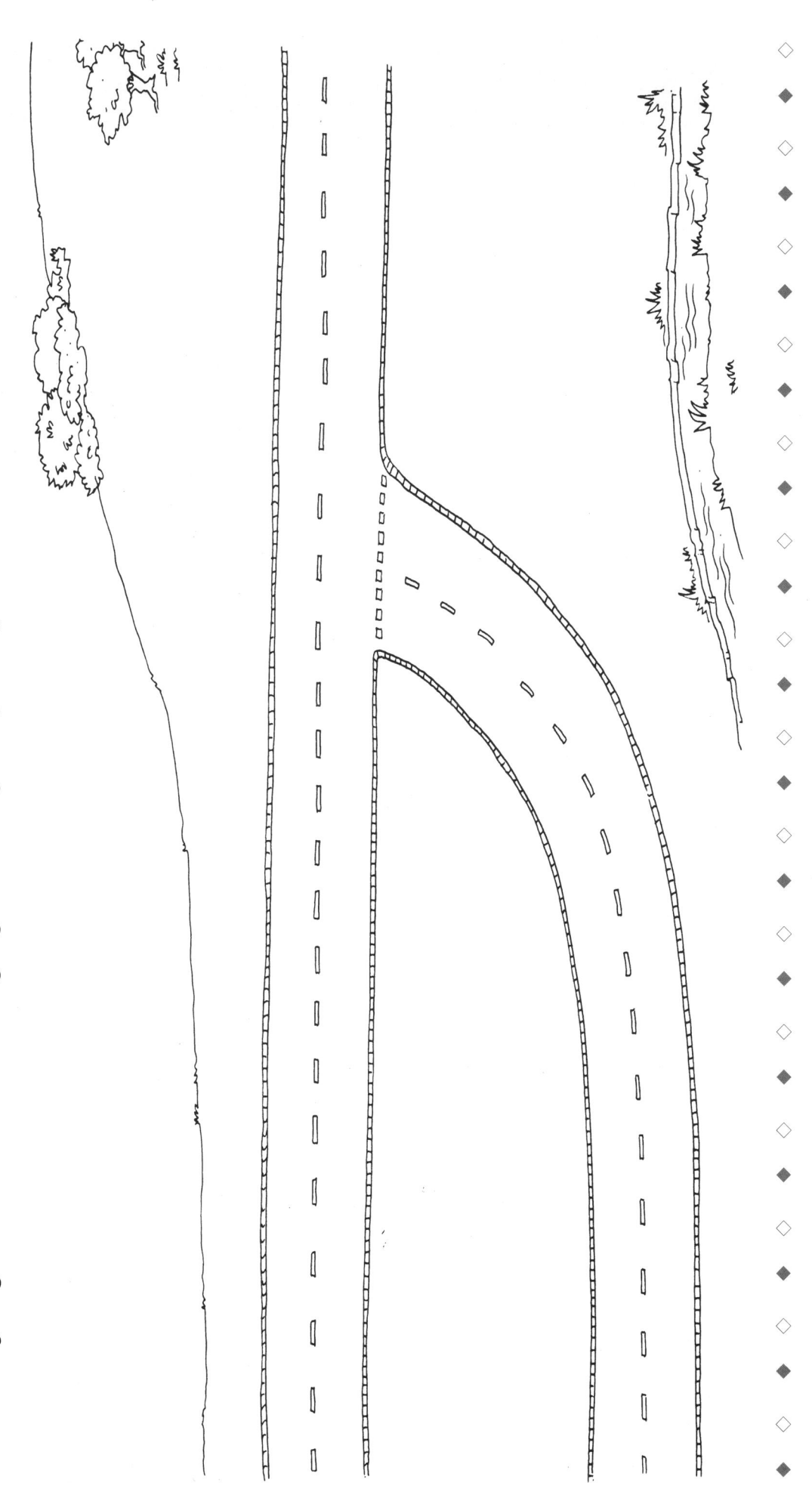

Hopscotch ◆ People and communities KS1/P1–3   PHOTOCOPIABLE PAGE   47

◆ What a community needs ◆

◆ A community needs housing and energy. Draw pictures to show other things that a community needs.

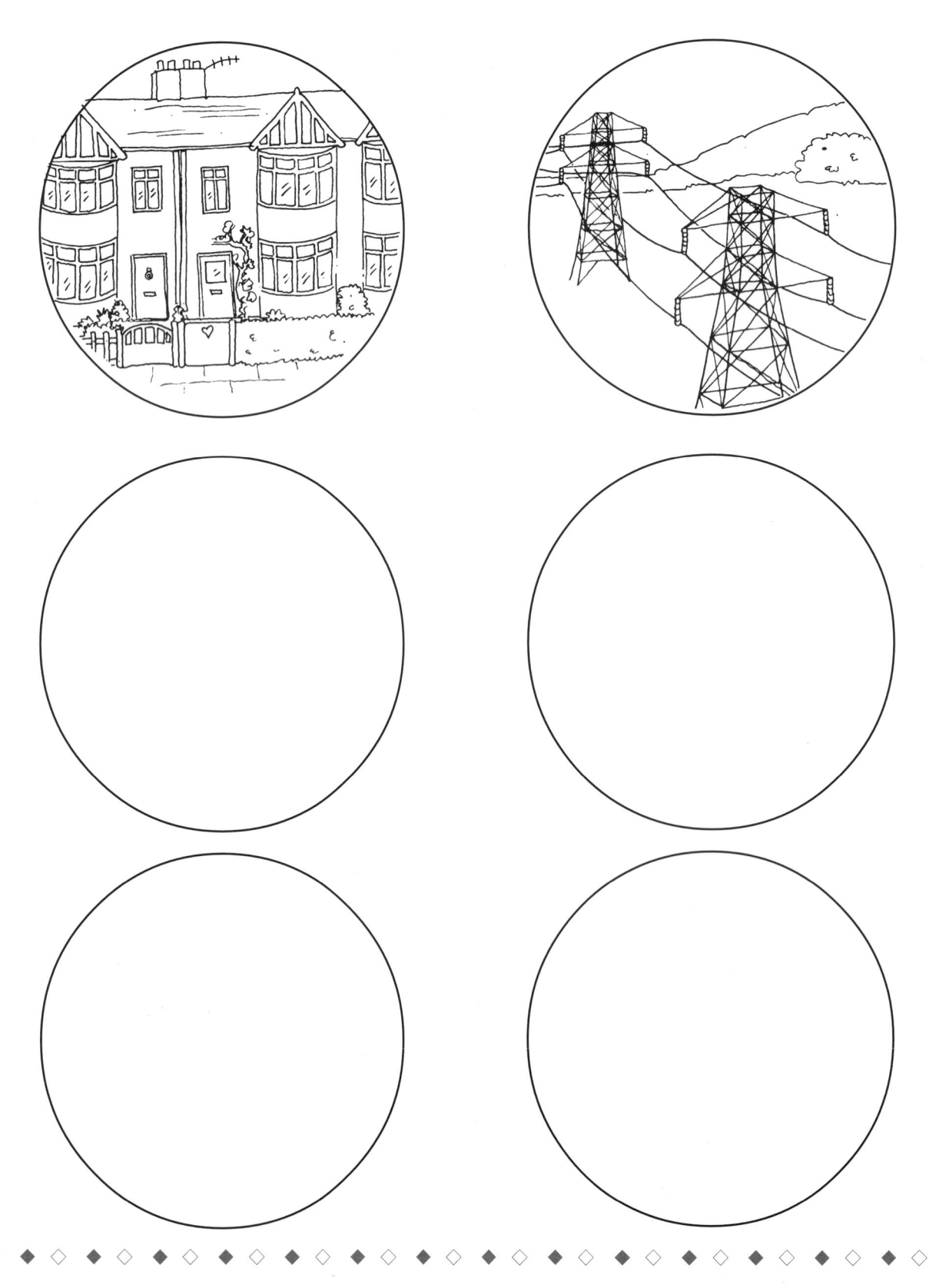

48   PHOTOCOPIABLE PAGE   Hopscotch ◆ People and communities KS1/P1–3